TRAINING
WITH
DISC

40 GAMES AND
TEAM BUILDING EXERCISES
TO LEAD YOUR
1ST OR 101ST
DISC WORKSHOP

DISC-U.ORG

Created as a resource learning center, DISC-U.org is centered on the education and application of the DISC Profile Assessment and enabling access to workshops, training material, online classes, videos and facilitator resources.

The Organization's goals are to:

1. Help everyone gain a better understanding of their unique behavioral style
2. Grow value for differences others bring
3. Enhance the ability to communicate better

Visit us online at www.DISC-U.org

ISBN-10: 0692380337
ISBN-13: 978-0692380338

Published by Focal Star Publishing, California, USA

Cover created by Mark Buschgens, Marked by Design, www.MarkedByDesign.net

Photo Credit: Tracey Hedge of Firefly Mobile Studios, www.Firefly2U.com

Editing Credit: Margaret Cantrell of Encouraging Word Publishing Services, www.MCeditor.com

TABLE OF CONTENTS

INTRODUCTION

I'm thrilled to see your interest in using DISC as a tool to help bring transformation into the lives of others! The power found in such a simple yet comprehensive assessment is astonishing. With just four measurement scales, a lot about each individual can be revealed. I'm truly thankful that you have now given me the opportunity to walk with you through the process of leading a DISC workshop.

I am a firm believer that DISC should be experienced more than it should be taught. Having led thousands through DISC Workshops in countless cities, states and countries, I have found one thing to be universally true — interactive exercises bring more value than static teachings.

Despite my best efforts to excite and energize participants with an emotionally moving and instructive teaching filled with powerful and potentially life-changing facts, figures and truths, students remember the revelations that come out of the exercises five to one. Having realized this years ago, I made a fundamental change in my teaching style. I now pack every workshop with as many exercises as I possibly can and limit my podium style lectures to an absolute minimum.

But Jason, exercises take up so much time! You can't cover nearly as much material as when you oversee the training process with a proper oration. And I would simply reply, "You are right."

I would, however, add that the purpose of the workshop isn't for me to show off everything I know about a topic, but for the student to learn something valuable about the topic. Their ability to learn and my ability to cover as much material as possible is forever locked into an inverse function where as one goes up, the other goes down.

With this revelation, I happily traded volume for value. My goal now isn't to cover as much as possible, but for the participants to truly learn something of value.

I'm guessing that you likely fit into one of three categories:

1. You're a professional trainer who has led hundreds of workshops
2. You've led several trainings or workshops at work or in a group setting
3. You're preparing to lead your first workshop

Regardless if you've led zero or a hundred DISC Workshops, this book will supply you with a foundation for leading an interactive workshop that thrills your participants and engages them in a deeper learning process that will see lasting results.

This book isn't intended to be a complete DISC resource. It will however, enable you to lead your first DISC workshop, and will provide more seasoned facilitators with additional exercises aimed at engaging the audience in the learning process.

In the next few sections I will share teaching tips, common questions and sample workshop schedules. Following that are 30 games and team building exercises that you can mix and match into a great combination that works for your audience and training preferences.

For the more experienced trainer with their own arsenal of DISC training tools, I think you will find several different exercises that will augment and spice up your own trainings to help bring the lessons to life by reinforcing participants' understanding of themselves and others — with a happy smile.

I hope you enjoy this resource and that we can connect sometime with an email about how your next DISC workshop goes. You can also join me online at www.DISC-U.org.

Jason Hedge

President and Founder of DISC-U.org

jasonh@DISC-U.org

Training with DISC

ABOUT DISC

The DISC Assessment is an indicator of behavioral tendencies.

It is HOW you do what you do. Of all of the internal forces going on in someone's head, DISC measures the one visible factor that is externally demonstrated — behaviors.

It began ages ago with Hippocrates studying what he called the four humors of the body. Galen then identified four temperaments; sanguine, melancholic, choleric and phlegmatic. William Marston identified ranges of behaviors and set them within the four scales of D, I, S and C. Walter Clarke later created an easily administered assessment, enabling us to easily identify our primary DISC types. Each level of development focused more and more on behaviors that were observable.

Observing behaviors enables you to immediately begin to learn something about everyone you meet. DISC provides a framework for understanding those behaviors to create reference points for that person's likely DISC style. The more you are able to observe, the more evidence you have that they will continue with those tendencies. Using behaviors enables you to develop strategies for how to interact with others without stopping them to ask for their assessment print out results.

The simplicity of DISC is also appealing. There are just four styles to learn about. Dominance, Influence, Steadiness and Conscientious. This enables participants to pick up the material quickly and begin to put it into action.

Someone with a higher *Dominance* scale than the other three demonstrates behaviors that can include:

- More hand gestures
- Is to the point
- Commands action
- Discusses deadlines
- Is known for being driven, focused, determined and confident

Someone with a higher *Influence* scale than the other three, demonstrates behaviors that can include:

- Constant body movement
- Optimistic focus
- Frequent discussions of people and feelings

- Lots of eye contact
- Is known for being outgoing, engaging and enthusiastic

Someone with a higher *Steadiness* scale than the other three, demonstrates behaviors that can include:

- Attentive listening
- Discusses agreement
- Uses "you" and "we" more than "I"
- Asks more "How" questions
- Is known for being patient, service oriented and reliable

Someone with a higher *Conscientious* scale than the other three, demonstrates behaviors that can include:

- Use of narrow gesturing
- Pauses thoughtfully before speaking
- Asks for agreement
- Asks more "Why" questions
- Is known for being detailed, deliberate and careful

We are each a unique mixture of the four scales. Our unique combination can set us apart, but the similarities we do have are enough to help us gain insight and understanding to help teams, couples, sales staff and organizations improve communication, reduce anxiety, increase trust and build connections.

Training with DISC

TIPS TO LEADING GREAT DISC WORKSHOPS

Start with the End in Mind

Adhering to Stephen Covey's book *7 Habits of Highly Effective People*, we should begin every workshop with the end in mind. You may want the group to learn to work together better, to provide better customer service, to increase sales or to improve their relationships or marriages. Above all that, I believe the ultimate goal of every DISC workshop participant is founded in these three areas:

1. Valuing yourself
2. Valuing others
3. Communicating better

When all three of these occur, you will have a solid foundation upon which to continue the building process. Without this foundation, many of the skills become activities to manipulate others toward our will. But, with a foundation based upon valuing ourselves and others, the tools learned with DISC enable us to work side-by-side to achieve greater things together.

It is also important as the workshop continues to integrate into the group discussions the value of focusing on behaviors, not intentions or emotions. Nine out of ten of us feel that we are really good at 'reading' others and knowing their intentions. But, how many times have we reacted harshly to someone when we incorrectly assumed their ill intentions, only to make the saying true — when you assume you make an 'a$$' out of 'u' and 'me' (ass-u-me). A great exercise to demonstrate this is the icebreaker called Silence. Give it a try, you'll enjoy it!

Finally, it is critical that the participants do not view DISC as a box or a way of defining their identity. DISC is all about behavioral *tendencies*. This means that they can change their behavior any time they would like. It takes extra energy to do it, but they can any time they choose to. I know highly administrative Is and outgoing Cs. During a workshop we are talking about generalities to help gain a basic understanding of this powerful tool. But, it is just one of the sets of tools out there to help understand others. Remember, this does not create boxes and does not define who they are or what they can do.

Preparation

All of the work you do behind the scenes is so that you don't have to overly work in front of everyone. You need to be fully present when you are on stage and when everything has been take care of, you can do your best to present.

Date, Time and Location

The preparation begins well before the workshop date. You'll need to arrange the date, the time and the room. The room should be larger than what is needed for a typical static group that just sits down all day since you will have them up and moving around during the exercises. Several of the activities will need the participants to gather around tables, which require more room than chairs.

Assessments

If you choose to use DISC Assessments with your workshop, you will need to coordinate with a vendor to get access to paper forms or online codes. The best assessments are paid online versions. They allow for customized reports tailored to each individual. However, when the budget is tight, the free assessments will at least identify the participant's primary DISC type. That is the majority of what you will be working with in these workshops anyway, so you should be fine. However, I do love a good comprehensive assessment, the kind where the participants come up afterwards and ask, semi-seriously, if I've been stalking them, because how else could the report know them so well? Those are fun moments.

Workbooks, Paper and Pens

Interactive workshops typically involve some need to write out responses to be shared later. Supplying pens and paper or notebooks is essential. Some of the exercises in this book include downloadable worksheets that you can use. You may consider including a binder or a folder to help participants keep everything together. My workshops have evolved so much that I actually created a workbook around the process, so that everything is bound in one place.

Presentation Slides

Projector and slides can help make a workshop come alive. For your first workshop, I wouldn't worry about preparing a Keynote or PowerPoint deck. But, as you continue to make your DISC Workshops more involved, adding slides and pictures can enhance the end user's experience. They also help to post up questions that the participants need to answer, so they don't need to quickly write them down at the beginning of each exercise. To use a projector, you'll need presenting software like Keynote or PowerPoint, a computer or device to run the presentation software, a projector, screen, electrical cords and audio/video connection cords. You may also want to purchase a wireless presenter or clicker so you can change slides without walking up to the computer or yelling, "Next!"

Microphones

Microphones are a must when working with large groups but in smaller groups I prefer to simply speak out loud. If you have difficulty projecting your voice to a level above the low rumble of workshop clamor, then a microphone may be best. The location where you are presenting may have microphones available and it is wise to check in advance. Wireless microphones work great if you like to talk a lot with your hands, you may want to see if an over-the-ear type is available. You may feel a bit like a cyborg, but it frees up your hands. Including a second microphone is great to help the entire audience hear a question from the audience or a team presenting from the front. If you don't use a microphone often, arrive at the meeting site early to try out the microphone. It can be off putting the first few times you hear yourself speaking through the speakers.

Water, Snacks and Facilities

Water, snacks and available restrooms make for a happy group. The first two aren't requirements, but if you are missing the third one it can get quite messy. You don't need to have a seven-course meal, but the more comfortable they are, the better they can focus on learning from you. It also steps up your game so they look forward to the next opportunity to train with you.

Marketing

Advertising for the event is another critical process that you don't want to miss. Setting the right expectations goes a long way. Building suspense and excitement will help garner their attention from the beginning. This is much easier than slowly earning it back during the workshop. Often times I will have the participants complete the online assessment but have the results come directly to me so they don't have a chance to see them. I let them know ahead of time that they will receive their printout during the first day of the workshop. I use this process to increase their curiosity and anticipation for the workshop. (It also helps them to focus during the Intro to DISC as they pay more attention to all of the types instead of just their own primary DISC type.) You don't need to spend a lot on marketing, but flyers and carefully crafted emails can go a long way in setting the audience up to be ready to learn. If you aren't a marketing genius, have someone else create the flyer for you. Online talent can be found at places like www.fiverr.com, www.odesk.com, www.elance.com, www.guru.com, www.freelancer.com to name just a few of the options.

Patience

Patience is one of the great skills that often eludes us. As the participants warm up to the idea that they get to stand up, move around and engage in the learning process, you will find that closing the exercises can become increasingly difficult. The problem is actually a good one though. You are enabling participants to actually participate! Add in patience and a microphone or booming voice, and eventually they will calm back down. Keep your cool and remember, they are learning and reinforcing what you are sharing when they talk. They just get carried away sometimes.

And if you are training a group of leaders, you may need an extra dose of patience. Leaders have a tendency to really enjoying these workshops, but they can have a difficult time realizing that they aren't running the workshop and should be focusing on you, the workshop leader. I typically put on a big smile and give them several notices to disperse the groups and find a seat. When you keep your cool and stay on track, you'll gain even more of their respect.

TIPS TO LEAD ENGAGING FOLLOW UP SESSIONS

Great facilitators (people like you) know that people are looking for more than a one-time experience. They are hungry for real change to take place. They need a lasting impression to be made that will help them continue to implement those changes.

Unfortunately, most training is viewed as an injection that is supposed to create immediate change. However, lasting change requires ongoing support and encouragement. It requires more than one contact point. It takes 20 days or more to create a new habit and lasting change requires more than one workshop.

The following exercises are the perfect tool to help your participants, clients and teams continue the reinforcement process to ensure that change really happens.

I highly recommend that when you set up a DISC Workshop, you build into your program one or more follow up trainings set at a later date. This will keep the information fresh in their minds, continue the learning process and ensure that the momentum you started with continues to build.

When you add follow up training to your proposal, you set yourself apart from other regular trainers. You demonstrate your commitment to the group and the value of DISC.
The follow up could be just one two-hour mini-session, or three 20 to 45 minute sessions spread across the next few months. It could be as brief as including an Icebreaker before a regular scheduled meeting. Regardless of the style, everyone will draw more value out of your training and DISC if you include additional follow up trainings.

Many professional trainers are thinking that's great, but it simply isn't cost effective! Well, you may be right. But, when there is a will, there is a way. If the economics just don't work out to revisit a site for such a brief time, find a trainer there to empower. Find someone on the team that is passionate about DISC and able to lead the group.

You could become the company's hero by spending a few minutes training them up in how to do the follow up training for you. With a short 15 minute meeting, you could create an advocate for you and for DISC and help the company with their follow up training system. The following exercises are often very easy to share about once they are understood, and can easily be led by passionate people that have never led a workshop before.

With the busyness of life, after your workshop you and your DISC training could be out of sight, out of mind. Follow up training is a way for you to be their resident expert. The hero that helped your DISC workshop stay on in the minds of the participants forever. Maximize the potential of this resource to help make a lasting difference.

Training with DISC

CREATING INTERACTIVE ENVIRONMENTS

Today's training environment is changing and evolving. There is more information immediately available online at the click of a button than what humanity has previously had access to for the last 2000 years. You can read or watch a video about nearly everything you could think of.

All of this learning potential — videos, blogs and online courses — is absent of one thing, deepened connections. Electronic mediums don't compare to genuine face-to-face interactions. There is a synergy that happens when people dialogue, plan, create and work together in the same room.

In addition, interactive workshops add a depth to learning that can't be gained by reading a book. Training tied to actual experience allows for more comprehensive learning. To emphasize this, think for a moment about who you would rather have as your next big city taxi driver; someone who got an A+ on the online driving test but has never driven before, or someone that has failed the online test three times but has been driving a taxi for seven years. Experience is ultimately more valuable.

Interactive workshops combine the best of training and experience together into one seamless process. It isn't hard to work them both together, but it is a different process than most of the training we've received. Most learning comes passively. We go somewhere, sit and watch, hear or read something and then we are done. Learning is conducted this way because it is efficient for the trainer. They can cover more information in a shorter amount of time when the audience just listens. By contrast, a trainer leading an interactive workshop won't be able to cover as many topics, but the audience will have a personal experience and a greater likelihood of implementing that knowledge. Which route do you feel is more effective?

As I discussed earlier, to create an engaging and interactive learning environment, you must be comfortable sacrificing the amount of content for the potential of a deeper learning experience.

Once you have effectively paired down the amount of content, you will focus in on the process of helping your audience to experience the items to be learned.

Step 1: Know your audience. Gain an understanding ahead of time as to what they know about DISC and what their past experience has been with it.

Step 2: Set expectations. Let your audience know in advance the topics you will cover and what outcomes you are anticipating for them.

Step 3: Plan for interaction. Ensure the meeting room has extra space for groups to spread out. Include extra tables for gathering teams for exercises. Choose from the exercises the activities that will create the learning experiences you are going after.

Step 4: Practice. It isn't easy to give up the microphone and let the audience follow an exercise while you essentially just watch. It is especially painful to sit quietly on stage when the audience is thinking or writing something out. You will want to keep talking, adding in additional facts, adding something, anything of value. But, it is just as important to lead from behind to ensure the audience receives the best experience possible. Practice with friends and family Practice learning patience by calmly gathering back everyone's attention when an exercise ends but the conversations don't. This practice will build the confidence to push through unfazed.

Step 5: Develop your wrap up. Of the two areas you will need to focus on, introducing exercises and wrapping them up, the second is the most powerful. This is where the countless 'aha' moments come from. After the fun of practicing and interacting is done, the wrap up locks in what was learned. The wrap up is best done by either:

- Asking questions to hear what the audience is gaining from the experience. This could include asking them what they are learning, asking them to summarize their experience or asking them about how they can apply what they just learned.
- Reviewing what previous groups have experienced during the exercise.
- Summarizing what has happened and what they have learned.

- Describing what advantages have come to those that have implemented what the audience has just learned.

After you've decided to create an interactive environment and you are coming to grips with the fact that you're trading quantity for quality, you are just about ready to begin.

Each of the exercises has a listed purpose. This creates the goal for the exercise and is the focal point for your wrap up time. When your audience emphasizes these points in their discussion, you know you've done your job.

Setting up the exercise is also important. Share this with energy and enthusiasm. You alone set the stage for the success of the exercise, so be sure to show how excited you are. This can feel foreign and fake, but is absolutely necessary. Even if you normally don't feel comfortable with a lot of expression, a lot is lost in transference from the stage to the audience. And the larger the audience, the larger the expressions and hand motions need to be to have any chance of reaching the audience. You are a performer, and this is the time to perform!

You also want to give them a reason to do what they will need to do, but without spelling out the purpose of the exercise. It is much better for them to come to an understanding of the value of the exercise themselves than for you to just give them the answer. Each exercise is different and although there are a few that you immediately jump into without an introduction, the rest require some set up.

To do this, create a reason for the participants to engage with each other:

- Competition is a powerful magnet to draw teams together.

- Setting a group goal also helps rally teams into action.

- Simple peer pressure works. Get one part of the group moving and the rest follow.

- Confidently directing the audience into action, knowing what you are doing, works wonders.

- Team building is a universally understood reason and is perfectly acceptable to use to initiate action.

- Learning opportunity is what most of them are their for, so when you need to be coy about the purpose, just emphasis it is another learning opportunity.

Once the exercise has begun, you shouldn't be very involved. You can answer a question here and there (unless you aren't supposed to according to the exercise instructions) or just step back and watch. Once I was able to let go of the control thing, I found out that I really enjoy watching what happens in each exercise. The patterns, similarities and sometimes differences between behaviors in different groups is mind-boggling.

After the first time or two, you will begin to catch the interactive training bug and won't want to go back to the monologue. It is such a powerful tool that it is hard to put down. Plus, you'll have as much fun as your audience! Simply focus on three main parts of interactive exercises, the intro, the exercise action time and the wrap up.

FEEDBACK

Be sure to ask for feedback on what the audience likes and what can be improved. Don't be afraid of a few stinging remarks. You can't make everyone happy, but you do want to learn from the experience. I prefer one page written feedback forms because they are easy to review, can be done by everyone at the end of the workshop and provide one more place for the audience to connect with you. Once collected, set the more positive responses in one pile, and the others in another. Quickly go through the second pile and read them quickly while looking for patterns. Don't get stuck on deeply reading them, but skim for honest and helpful input. Write out any patterns you see and then throw them away. Then go through the positive responses. Look for patterns and any contradictory statements that can cancel out any negative patterns. Pull out any testimonials to share with others later and hold on to the positive ones to review later.

I've included a sample evaluation form in the online accessible material that you are free to modify and use as your own. We all want to get better and like it or not, feedback is the way to know how to grow.

TRAINING
WITH
DISC

COMMON
DISC
QUESTIONS

There are oodles of questions that come up before, during and after a workshop. These are a few of the most common ones I have encountered that I feel warrant review here.

Q How does the understanding of DISC bring value to a relationship or organization?

A When someone understands their own style and then identifies the value of someone else's style, it allows them to stop measuring others by their own way of doing things. It also enables them to create opportunities for other styles to be successful based upon individual styles and strengths.

Q Is certification required to facilitate DISC workshops?

A No, it is not a requirement. However, the more training you have, the better equipped you are to answer participant's questions. Numerous vendors offer training courses and materials such as the DISC Facilitator Training Kit.

Q Does maturing with DISC mean that the scores for each of the four scales all increase to the top?

A Maturity within the realms of DISC enables your participants to understand how they are wired and to be comfortable being themselves wherever they are. They also know when and how to change their behavior when necessary to respond to a need.

Q Doesn't DISC just put people into boxes?

A The 'box' that some feel DISC forces people into really isn't there. DISC measures behavioral *tendencies*, not behavioral laws. DISC simply helps us to understand those tendencies in a way that enables greater understanding, better communication and increased connection.

Q Which is the best DISC type to have?

A Your type is the best for you to have. If you kept changing your behaviors to match up to another style, you wouldn't feel like you and it would be exhausting. When both you and your environment accept you for who you are, then you'll realize that there isn't a better type to be.

Q What is a quick way to describe DISC to someone that has never heard of DISC?

A DISC helps describe HOW we do what we do. It's an assessment that measures behavioral tendencies. DISC has four scales that measures factors titled; dominance, influence, steadiness and conscientious.

Q What other names and analogies have been used in place of D-I-S-C?

A Several variations have been delivered over time including:

- Temperaments; Sanguine, Melancholic, Choleric and Phlegmatic
- Different words in the DISC acronym; Driven, Decisive, Inspirational, Interactive, Stabilizing, Steady, Compliance, Cautious.
- Colors; Red, Yellow, Green and Blue
- Different variations of animals, birds, gems and more

Q How much does someone's DISC style change over the years?

A Generally, there is very little change that happens in someone's DISC profile, especially when they take a high quality assessment each time. But there can be times when a DISC profile genuinely changes, such as after a dramatic life event or after someone comes into a new level of emotional healing.

Q How much time should pass between taking DISC assessments?

A I would suggest waiting at least a year in most cases. Unless something significant has happened in the year, the results are not likely to indicate anything new.

Q If your DISC profile doesn't change much over someone's life, why would you want to take the assessment again?

A You may not ever need to. But there are some comprehensive assessments that provide additional information on areas that do change, which can be very helpful. This could include comparing your natural and your adapted styles. It is also a way to refresh your memory about your results.

Q Can DISC profiles be used in the hiring process?

A Some can. Only assessments that have proven validity and reliability studies done should be used as one part of a hiring process. There are numerous vendors for DISC assessments and they can provide the results to those studies if they have done them.

Q Do different cultures have higher percentages of some DISC types than other cultures?

A Statistically, there are only minor differences. Across the world, there are the same percentages of Ds, Is, Ss and Cs. Ss have the highest percentage followed by Is, Ds and Cs.

Training with DISC

SAMPLE WORKSHOP SCHEDULES

There are millions of different combinations of exercises that can be used when presenting DISC. It all depends upon the audience, the time, the location, resources and the expected outcome.

I have found that a basic tempo of mixing training and exercises helps the audience to stay engaged and to deepen their understanding of the material. Here are a few examples based upon length of time with <u>included exercises underlined</u>. I have suggested a few of the training session topics, but feel free to insert in any of your own trainings that you know work best.

Suggested First DISC Workshop Schedule

This is where I would suggest starting for your first workshop. It is short, sweet and to the point. Your participants will learn a lot and have a great time with the engaging exercises.

- 5 minutes   Intro
- 20 minutes   Icebreaking Exercise: Tallest Tower
- 30 minutes   Training: Intro to DISC
- 45 minutes   Reinforcing Exercise: Coat of Arms
- 15 minutes   Break
- 40 minutes   Reinforcing Exercise: Valuable

1/2 Day Training

- 5 minutes   Intro
- 10 minutes   Icebreaking Exercise: Silence
- 30 minutes   Training: Intro to DISC
- 45 minutes   Reinforcing Exercise: How We are Misunderstood
- 15 minutes   Break
- 45 minutes   Reinforcing Exercise: Builders & Finishers
- 30 minutes   Training
- 45 minutes   Reinforcing Exercise: Complement Face Off

1/2 Day Training

- 5 minutes — Intro
- 35 minutes — Icebreaking Exercise: How I Lead
- 30 minutes — Training: Intro to DISC
- 45 minutes — Reinforcing Exercise: Managing Types
- 15 minutes — Break
- 25 minutes — Reinforcing Exercise: Priorities
- 30 minutes — Training
- 45 minutes — Reinforcing Exercise: Leadership Scenario

3/4 Day Training

- 5 minutes — Intro
- 30 minutes — Icebreaking Exercise: Blind Communication
- 30/10 min — Take Assessment and/or Review Results
- 30 minutes — Training: Intro to DISC
- 20 minutes — Break
- 45 minutes — Reinforcing Exercise: Marketing Team
- 90 minutes — Lunch
- 15 minutes — Icebreaking Exercise: Change Around Us
- 35 minutes — Training
- 45 minutes — Reinforcing Exercise: Dream Job

1 Day Training

- 5 minutes   Intro
- 30 minutes   <u>Icebreaking Exercise: Tallest Tower</u>
- 30/10 min   Take Assessment and/or Review Results
- 30 minutes   <u>Training: Intro to DISC</u>
- 20 minutes   Break
- 45 minutes   <u>Reinforcing Exercise: Coat of Arms</u>
- 90 minutes   Lunch
- 10 minutes   <u>Icebreaking Exercise: Silence</u>
- 40 minutes   Training
- 45 minutes   <u>Reinforcing Exercise: Motivators and Anxiety Producers</u>
- 15 minutes   Break
- 40 minutes   Training
- 45 minutes   <u>Reinforcing Exercise: Panel Q&A</u>
- 25 minutes   <u>Reinforcing Exercise: Accountability Partners</u>

1 Day Training

- 5 minutes   Intro
- 35 minutes   <u>Icebreaking Exercise: Ideal Vehicle</u>
- 30/10 min   Take Assessment and/or Review Results
- 30 minutes   <u>Training: Intro to DISC</u>
- 20 minutes   Break
- 45 minutes   <u>Reinforcing Exercise: Blind Spots</u>
- 90 minutes   Lunch
- 25 minutes   <u>Icebreaking Exercise: Silent Video Chat</u>
- 40 minutes   Training

- 45 minutes   Reinforcing Exercise: Leadership Scenario
- 15 minutes   Break
- 40 minutes   Training
- 35 minutes   Reinforcing Exercise: Difficult Dealings

3 Day Training

(Modified from the *DISC Facilitator Training Kit* as an example of combining trainings and exercises)

Day 1

- 45 minutes   Registration
- 15 minutes   Welcome & Outline
- 30 minutes   Icebreaking Exercise: Tallest Tower
- 30 minutes   Break
- 45 minutes   Training: Intro to DISC (Expanded)
- 45 minutes   Reinforcing Exercise: Motivators and Anxiety Producers
- 90 minutes   Lunch
- 45 minutes   Reinforcing Exercise: Coat of Arms
- 30 minutes   Exercise: Unpacking DISC
- 30 minutes   Break
- 45 minutes   Reinforcing Exercise: Builders and Finishers

Day 2

- 45 minutes   Open Discussion & Networking
- 15 minutes   Welcome
- 45 minutes   Training: Leadership Aptitudes

- 30 minutes   Break
- 30 minutes   Exercise: Understanding Your Aptitudes & Descriptors
- 45 minutes   Reinforcing Exercise: Leadership Scenario
- 90 minutes   Lunch
- 30 minutes   Training: Communicating Primary DISC Types
- 45 minutes   Training: Natural vs. Adapted Style
- 30 minutes   Break
- 35 minutes   Reinforcing Exercise: Difficult Dealings

Day 3

- 45 minutes   Open Discussion & Networking
- 15 minutes   Welcome
- 45 minutes   Training: Team DISC Wheel
- 30 minutes   Break
- 45 minutes   Training: Bringing DISC Home
- 30 minutes   Exercise: Aptitude Team Graph
- 90 minutes   Lunch
- 20 minutes   Training: DISC Communication
- 40 minutes   Exercise: DISC Communication
- 15 minutes   Reinforcing Exercise: Quick Reference
- 35 minutes   Reinforcing Exercise: Application
- 30 minutes   Break
- 40 minutes   Conclusion and Q&A

GETTING STARTED

Just in case you haven't already created your own DISC trainings, I've included the first and most important one for you. *Intro to DISC* shares an overview of each type and helps increase your participant's awareness of how amazing they are and how amazing the other three types are in their own right.

The exercises are broken down into two categories, Icebreakers and Reinforcing Exercises. Icebreakers are great at getting participants to loosen up and begin to interact. They also work great to break off the sleepy feeling after lunch and to re-engage the group. The Reinforcing Exercises are designed to either follow a training to reinforce the main points, or as a learning tool by itself as you let them learn during the exercise and then conclude the exercise by summarizing what they have learned.

Each exercise contains several sections;

- **Purpose** describes the intended outcome

- **Overview** gives you a quick look at what happens during the exercise

- **Prerequisite** lets you know if you should provide any training before using the exercise because the participants will need that knowledge to do the exercise

- **Materials** list what you will need to collect ahead of time to complete the exercise

- **Preparation** tells you if there is something that you will need to do before starting the exercise

- **Time** lets you know roughly how long the entire exercise will take. With a larger group it could take more time. If you have a smaller group it could take less time. As you become more comfortable with the material, you may need to fight to keep these timeframes.

- **Time Line** gives you a breakdown of how much time is roughly spent on each part of the exercise

- **Instructions** break down the process into easy to follow steps. They intentionally leave lots of room for you to add in your personality and training style

- **Alternative Options** help you create new versions of the exercises to keep things fresh and new

- **Tips** include additional thoughts to keep in mind while running the exercises to ensure they end up well

I've included three bonus exercises just for fun. *Application, Interrupting* and the *Quick Reference* exercises are fun and powerful. The *Application* exercise helps to drive home everything you've worked on during the workshop by creating an action plan to put what they have learned into cation. The *Interrupting* exercise helps the Ds and Is to realize that they can receive more helpful input if they pause periodically. Ss and Cs then realize that it is ok to interrupt a high D or I when you are adding in valuable information. Ds and Is get charged up with it! And the *Quick Reference* exercise includes a link to a downloadable PDF that helps the participant easily create a quick reference guide to there own behavioral style. This can help them remember vital information, but it also can be posted to help others realize how to best connect and communicate with each other.

Training with DISC

TRAINING WITH DISC 10

GENERAL TIPS

When first starting out, it may seem as though the training times and introductions to the exercises will go by faster than planned. Although many of us end up talking a bit faster when we are nervous, it is much easier to go over the time than to end early. As you become more comfortable with the material you will definitely find this to be true. Asking more questions during the wrap up time can get the audience re-engaged after the exercise and allow them to externally process what they are learning together.

When working with very large groups, to reduce the time spent in multiple team presentations, you can:

- Make a game out of setting a hard time limit where you have other participants help you count down the final seconds each team has to present.

- If you have a large audience with multiple similar type groups, you can have them flip a coin to see who will present instead of having every team present similar material for each exercise.

On another note, if you have a smaller group and don't have several people in each DISC type group, you can skip that group, disperse the one or two people among their secondary DISC type groups and stand in their place to highlight what that group would have said. You can also add yourself to that small group, or ask for volunteers that have that type as a secondary type.

ICEBREAKERS

Training with DISC

SILENCE

Purpose: To help everyone to understand the difference between guessing at someone's intentions or thoughts and focusing on behaviors they can experience.

Overview: After a brief introduction, don't say anything for 30 seconds. Everyone feels the awkwardness build before you release the tension by announcing it was an exercise. Ask the audience what you did during that time of silence and slowly focus the conversation toward your behaviors.

Prerequisite: None.

Materials: None.

Preparation: None.

Time: 10-15 minutes.

Time Line: 5 seconds – Greet and share your name.

30 seconds – Don't talk for a full 30 seconds.

4-9 minutes – Ask questions of audience.

5 minutes – Wrap up.

Instructions:

1. Start with a very brief introduction: "Hello, my name is Jane Doe and what we will be discussing today will forever improve the way you communicate and connect with others. I want to share one of the most important ideas of today..."

2. Don't say anything for at least 30 seconds. During this time you are thinking about something they will never be able to guess, like dressing up in a monkey suit and selling bananas at the fair. You can look across the room at each of the participants, or you can simply stare off in thought up at the ceiling.

3. Break the silence by thanking them for their patience and ask the audience, "What behaviors did you observe during this time of silence?"

   a. Responses may include, standing, not talking, pacing, nothing, etc.

4. Ask the audience, "What was I thinking about during that time of silence?"

   a. Responses may include, skiing, dancing, eating cake, nothing.

5. Conclude by congratulating them on identifying the behaviors correctly, but point out that no one was correct about identifying your thoughts.

6. Ask them what happens when we try to identify some else's thoughts or intentions.

    a. Responses may include; we get it wrong, we make wrong decisions, and the eventual response: "we assume, and we all know what happens when you assume something — you make an 'a$$' out of 'u' and 'me.'" (ass-u-me).

7. Transition them back to the value of focusing on behaviors and lead them into the introduction of DISC, the focus on behavioral tendencies and hint toward the wisdom of focusing on behaviors rather than guessing at their thoughts and intentions.

Alternate Options: Instead of just standing on stage you could pace, you could intentionally look each participant in the eye, you could walk around the inside of the building, you could furiously take notes on something important. Any of these will cause the audience to feel uncomfortable and help you accomplish your goal.

Tips: You'll be amazed at how awkward the pausing part can be the first couple of times! As a presenter, it is difficult to figure out how to do nothing while everyone waits for you and becomes uncomfortable with you. Practice how long 30 seconds of silence really is. It can be hard but the lesson learned in the end is worth it!

Training with DISC

TALLEST TOWER

Overview: Break the group up into evenly distributed mixed type teams of 6-12. Have each team gather around a table and wait for instructions. Briefly give vague instructions about building the tallest tower. Increase the tension by counting down the time. Close by focusing their attention on the behaviors of those on the team.

Purpose: To shift their focus toward observable behaviors and the different approaches others take to the same challenge.

Prerequisite: Purchase and arrange all of the material to quickly distribute to each team's table.

Materials:

- One bag of large marshmallows per team.
- One box of coffee stir sticks per team.
- One plastic mat or plastic table cloth per team.
- One bag of round candies (i.e. Peppermint Starlights, M&Ms, Skittles) to share between the teams.
- Clean table top for each team.
- Timer.

Preparation: Group the materials for even distribution to each team. Only one candy is needed for each team.

Time: 20-35 minutes depending upon how much time you give the teams to complete the towers (and sometimes to rebuild them) and how much time you spend interacting with the participants afterwards.

Time Line: 5 minutes – Introduce exercise and break into teams.

10-15 minutes – Tower building time.

5-15 minutes – Wrap up.

Instructions:

1. Share that this exercise is a competition to see which team can build the tallest tower. Find a table with no more than (6-12) people and then I will give you the instructions.

2. Once they are at the tables, with the materials situated, give them the instructions, "I will only share these instructions once. Using only the stir sticks and marshmallows, build the tallest tower. The tower must be free standing and sit on the tablecloth on

the table. The candy must be at the very top of the tower. You have ten minutes, go!"

3. Then walk around the tables encouraging them and periodically announcing to the group how much time is remaining.

4. Countdown the last two minutes and also the final seconds. (But, you can add more tower building time if necessary and time allows.)

5. Once time is up, have them begin to write down all of the behaviors they observed of the others on their team.

6. Wrap up by announcing the winning team, and asking what behaviors they witnessed. Focus on the different behaviors of their team members.

7. Close by mentioning that it is important to focus on behaviors, versus attitudes and intentions, since that is what DISC is all about.

(Be warned that this can be a messy exercise, leaving residue on table and hands! You may want to purchase hand wipes or allow time to wash up in the restroom.)

Alternate Options: Using the same materials, reconstruct the leaning tower of Pisa that leans, but doesn't fall over. Or build the Eiffel Tower or Statue of Liberty. The judging would be more subjective with these, but the real focus of the exercise is to create an activity that allows them to see real behaviors in action.

Tips: This is one of my favorite workshop openers. It lets the group know that this training is going to be different and engages them in the learning process. Increase the audience's competitiveness by offering a prize and counting down the remaining time, especially the last few minutes and the final seconds.

Training with DISC

BLIND
COMMUNICATION

Overview: One person from each mixed type team views a design of colored shapes and while wearing a blindfold helps their team build the same design.

Purpose: To reinforce the understanding that communication isn't always received the same way as the sender intends it to be.

Prerequisite: None.

Materials:

- One printed picture of a pre-designed configuration of colored shapes as a template.
- One envelope for each team of 4 to 12 people with the same colored shapes used with the template.
- One blindfold for each team's Communicator.
- Timer.

Preparation: Create a template using colored shapes and take a picture or hide your template so only the Communicators see it. Create an envelope with the same colored shapes as the template for each team.

Time: 30 minutes.

Time Line: 5 minutes – Introduce exercise and break into teams.

2 minutes – Show one leader from each group the template.

13 minutes – Allow blindfolded 'Communicator' to lead team through build process.

10 minutes – Wrap up.

Instructions:

1. Break the group up into mixed type teams of 4-12.
2. Have each team select one person as the 'Communicator.'
3. Meet privately with the communicators and show them the template of colored shapes that you've prepared. Give them an envelope with the same set of colored shapes and a blindfold. Have them return to their team without talking.
4. Instruct the group to blindfold each Communicator. Those people will now describe how to arrange the colored shapes in the envelope the same way as the template. The communicator is not allowed to see

their team's progress and cannot help other than by talking.

5. Wrap up the exercise by showing everyone what the template looked like and congratulating the teams.

6. Ask the Communicators how the process felt to them; where they thought it went well and where it did not. Then ask the teams the same questions.

7. Close by discussing that even though we can picture something in our head, it isn't easy to communicate it in a way so that others can see it the same way. Different people think, act and communicate differently.

Alternate Options: To make the exercise even harder, you can take some of the larger shapes in your template and cut them into smaller shapes. Now the teams must figure out how to combine them to make the same that the Communicator is describing. i.e. Cut a diamond shape in half to make two triangles.

Tips: Take a picture to show to the Communicators and later to show or project on a screen to the participants to compare their arrangement with your template.

Training with DISC

2 X 2 X 2

Overview: Break up into pairs. Each person shares 2 areas that others have mentioned that you do well in and 2 areas you are aware of where improvement could help.

Purpose: To encourage group interaction and conversations that reinforce our strengths and enable us to recognize areas for improvement.

Prerequisite: None.

Materials: None.

Preparation: None.

Time: 20 minutes.

Time Line: 5 minutes – Introduce exercise and break into pairs.

5 minutes – Discuss strengths.

5 minutes – Discuss weaknesses.

5 minutes – Wrap up.

Instructions:

1. Ask everyone to stand up, move around and find someone you do not already know well. The two of you will have several minutes each to share about two areas where you have received compliments and praise from others about something you do well. Then, after both of you have shared, follow up with two areas that you know you could use some improvement. If you finish early, ask the other person to describe one practical step they could take in the next few days to begin to bring improvement in one of those two areas.

2. Help guide their time by letting them know when they should be working on the second half of the task.

3. Close by asking for a show of hands where a pair had one or more strengths or weaknesses in common.

4. Follow by asking if any of the pairs had a strength in the area where the other had a weakness. Discuss if they feel comfortable and then discuss the potential for every organization or relationship to improve if we actively helped others by applying our strengths to cover another's weaknesses and asked for help covering our own.

Alternate Options: You could start them off with something easier such as their top two favorite movies, TV shows, board games, candies or pies.

Tips: Don't be afraid to jump into the mix and bounce around between the groups to listen in and share a bit about yourself.

Training with DISC

HOW I LEAD

Overview: Answer questions about your own leadership style, then get into groups and discuss how you lead. What similarities do you have with others? What differences?

Purpose: To encourage group interaction and conversations focused on everyone's leadership style and the different approaches.

Prerequisite: None.

Materials: None. But you may consider projecting the questions on a screen, writing them on a whiteboard or printing them on a handout.

Preparation: Possibly. (See suggestions above.)

Time: 35 minutes.

Time Line: 10 minutes – Introduce exercise and time to answer questions.

　　　　　　　20 minutes – Share answers.

　　　　　　　5 minutes – Wrap up.

Instructions:

1.　Share that throughout your life, you've had several different leaders that managed in different ways. Can you describe your leadership style? Answer the following questions on your own and afterwards we will get into groups of four to share, compare and contrast your responses.

　　▫ How I Lead:

　　a. What is your favorite part about being a leader?

　　b. When leading a team, what do you do to get them started and motivated to do a good job?

　　c. What is your preferred method to stay connected with the group after things get started?

　　d. How do you address when someone on the team makes a big mistake?

　　e. How do you ensure new team members are brought up to speed on a project?

　　f. If you must be away from the team for an extended period of time, what happens to the productivity of the team?

　　g. What do you like least about being a leader?

2. Wrap up by asking if anyone had any 'Aha' moments about their leadership style during this exercise or if anyone would like to share something they learned about themselves.

3. Close by generalizing some of the differences you heard between the different leadership styles, and although they may be different from person to person, each style can be very effective.

Alternate Options: You could end the Wrap Up section by directing the focus to their team and ask if each person has preferences in how they like to be led. After a few have shared, you can summarize and point out that each person wants to be led in a different way. The more a leader understands about DISC, the better equipped they are to meet each of their team's needs.

Tips: When you hear of several different ideas that seem to be polar opposites, be sure to not place any value on them, but simply show different styles have worked for different people.

Training with DISC

TRAINING WITH DISC 16

SILENT VIDEO CHAT

Purpose: To energize the participants and get them focusing on behaviors.

Overview: Break the group up into evenly distributed mixed type teams of 4-12. Secretly show a set of behaviors to the first person who passes it along to the next person and so on until the last person demonstrates the message they received which is compared to the original.

Prerequisite: None.

Materials: None.

Preparation: Create a set of hand movements that you will show to one person from each team and will repeat at the end of the exercise.

Time: 25 minutes.

Time Line: 5 minutes – Introduce exercise, break into teams and secretly show one person from each team the set of hand motions.

10 minutes – Set of hand motions are shared one at a time to the entire team.

10 minutes – Wrap up.

Instructions:

1. Break the group up into mixed type groups of 4-12.

2. Let them know that they will be playing an updated version of the old school game called Telephone.

3. Have them stand in a line facing the back of the room, and pull the first person from each team to another area out of sight. Demonstrate (or show a video) of a set of hand movements and then repeat the same set one more time.

4. Have everyone rejoin their teams without talking. Inform the group that you've given an urgent message that absolutely must make it to the last person, but the sound didn't work during the video chat, so you used a specific set of hand movements.

5. Have the teams line up all facing the back of the room. The first person then shares the message with the second person who then turns and taps the third person on the shoulder. Repeat until the message reaches the end of the line.

6. No one can talk during the exercise.

7. Bring up the last person in each team and have them all demonstrate the message to the group at the same time. Ask the group if any of them looked alike.

8. Then show them what the original message of hand signals looked like. Who do they think did the best?

9. Ask the group how their experience was. What was easy about this? What was difficult? Highlight that behaviors are an important part of our everyday lives and yet we don't always pay the attention to them that we could.

Alternate Options: You could also allow the team to only talk and not use any hand motions as they describe what the hand motions were. This helps focus on the value of clear communication.

You could also allow some teams to only talk and other teams to only use hand motions. If you are feeling devious, you could give different sets of hand motions to the teams that talk to help confuse the non-talking teams.

Tips: I prefer to use a video of the set of hand signals rather than peform them each time. This allows me to discretly show the first group the signals and ensures consistency. I have a copy on my phone to show the first group and then I use Keynote to share the same video to the entire group at the end.

Training with DISC

LIFELINE

Purpose: To energize the participants and encourage group interaction.

Overview: Break the group up into evenly distributed mixed type teams of 4-12. The first team to move the marble from one end of the room to the other and drop it in the bucket before the rest wins.

Prerequisite: None.

Materials:

- Three pieces of PVC pipe 1.5 to 2 feet in length per team.
- One marble that rolls freely through the pipe per team.
- One bucket per team.

Preparation: Group pipes, marbles and bucket for each team.

Time: 25 minutes.

Time Line: 5 minutes – Introduce exercise and break into teams.

10 minutes – Lifeline exercise.

10 minutes – Wrap up.

Instructions:

1. Split the group into teams of 4-12.

2. Excitedly share with the group that this is a matter of life and death! This marble represents life saving supplies that must be moved from the supply warehouse to the paramedics at the other end of the room.

3. Share that they must work as a team to move the marble from one end of the room to the other as fast as possible.

4. Then share the guidelines, "You can only use the supplied transportation tubes to touch the marble, because the supplies are ruined if they touch anything else.

5. Tell them that your team must start over if:

    a. The marble falls or touches anything other than pipe after starting.

    b. Someone holds the pipe at either end.

c. Someone walks or moves the pipe horizontally when his or her pipe possesses the marble.

6. State that the paramedics are counting on you to bring them these critical supplies!

7. Line up the teams and let them put the marble in the first tube just before you say go.

8. Encourage each team, but have them start over if they violate any of the rules.

Alternate Options: You could create the teams where everyone has the same DISC type. You could also only allow them to use one hand on the pipe at a time.

Tips: Find a good balance of fun and good sportsmanship by requiring restarts early in the game where it is easier to restart.

Training with DISC

ANIMALIZED

Overview: Show a picture of numerous types of animals and ask everyone to select one of the animals and then discuss with a partner about a quality they possess that is similar to some aspect of that animal.

Purpose: To encourage group interaction and conversations focused on how different we each are.

Prerequisite: None.

Materials: None.

Preparation: None.

Time: 15 minutes.

Time Line: 5 minutes – Introduce exercise and break into pairs.

   5 minutes – Each person shares.

   5 minutes – Wrap up.

Instructions:

1. Show an image or pass out a flyer that has numerous different animals on it.

2. Ask the audience to select one of the animals and then describe a quality they and the animal both have in common.

3. Ask everyone to stand up, move around and find someone you do not already know well. The two of you will have five minutes to share which animal you selected and then describe the quality you possess that is similar to an aspect of that animal.

4. Follow up by picking one of the animals and asking a few people to share why they picked that animal.

5. Close by focusing on the differences of each person even when they chose the same animal.

Alternate Options: You could ask them to pick two animals and a different quality they have in common with each. You could also ask their partner to pick an animal and have the other pick a quality they have in common with that animal.

Tips: Remind participants that they cannot be wrong and to have fun with this process.

TRAINING WITH DISC 19

CHANGE AROUND US

Overview: Participants will pair up with someone they don't know well. Give everyone one minute to observe each other. Then they each turn around and change one or two things about themselves. They then face each other and try to identify the changes on their partner. Discussion follows with how they felt and how quickly all of the changes come back to their normal state.

Purpose: To encourage group interaction and conversations focused on behaviors. Reinforces understanding that some people are more comfortable with change than others.

Prerequisite: None.

Materials: None.

Preparation: None.

Time: 15 minutes.

Time Line: 5 minutes – Introduce exercise and break into pairs.

2 minutes – First partner makes changes and other guesses.

2 minutes – Second partner makes changes and other guesses.

5 minutes – Discussion.

Instructions:

1. Ask everyone to stand up, to move about the room and pair up with someone that they don't already know very well.

2. Once everyone has paired up, they face each other for a minute and then they both turn back to back. The first person changes three things about themself and they both turn around and the second person tries to guess what those three items were.

3. Then they both turn back to back. The second person changes three things about themself and they both turn around and now the first person tries to guess what those three items were.

4. After a few minutes, calm the group and have each pair talk about how they felt.

5. Follow up by asking a few pairs to share with the group how they felt.

6. Ask them to also discuss how quickly everyone in the room put their changed items back in place.

Alternate Options: You could have both people change three things each at the same time.

Tips: If some groups end up with three people, this exercise will work just as well.

TRAINING

Training with DISC

INTRO
TO
DISC

Overview: Introduce the four primary DISC types and give a foundation for the overall workshop objective of understanding the basics of DISC.

Purpose: To help everyone feel great about their own primary DISC type and begin to see the value in each of the other DISC types.

Prerequisite: None.

Materials: None.

Preparation: None.

Time: 30 minutes.

Time Line: 30 minutes – Training on the four primary DISC types.

Instructions:

(This section is more robust than any of the other sets of instructions providing additional in depth guidance to help you feel as confident as possible leading your first DISC workshop. Please review this section thoroughly so you do not simply read this information to your audience. Know it and passionately share it!)

1. Explain that DISC is one of the many tools that helps describe the uniqueness within each person, but it is the best one to describe the universally understood dynamic of behavior — something we do everyday, all day long.

2. Share that it also represents an aspect of us that applies to life as well as work. Behaviors are what we get paid to do at work, so DISC is a great tool to use in the work environment as well as any area focusing on getting tasks done or interacting with people.

3. Discuss what DISC is not:

    a. NOT a test because there is not right or wrong. There isn't a best style or a good or bad style. Each one is valuable and different.

    b. NOT a personality test. It doesn't measure your psychological makeup, your intelligence, emotional quotient or your "dating-worthiness" index.

    c. NOT a box. DISC is not intended to be used as a labeling system to define the limits and capabilities of people.

d. Not your identity. It doesn't define who you are or what you can do.

4. Share what DISC is:

a. IS the measurement of behavioral tendencies. Given the same situation, you will naturally react the same way over and over and over again. You can consciously choose to react differently, but if you don't have to, you rarely will.

b. IS a predictor. You can use the DISC profile to predict the likely response someone will have in a given particular situation.

c. IS a reference. You can begin to understand other's behavioral styles and similar outcomes based upon the type of input and their style.

d. IS a four letter acronym. The letters D – I – S – C each represent a scale measuring out the four dynamics of DISC.

5. D is for the scale of Dominance. I is for the scale of Influence. S is for the scale of Steadiness. C is for the scale of Conscientious.

6. Discuss that everyone has a little of each of the four styles. They may notice a little of themselves in each area, but there will be one or possibly two that you really identify with.

7. Disclose that when discussing these types, you are discussing them as if the person is purely 100% just that type and 0% any other type. That combo just simply doesn't exist and therefore no one is exactly like the terms or examples you share.

8. Introduce the four types. Be sure to show enthusiasm for all four types evenly.

9. High D:

a. Someone scoring high on the D scale is compelled, driven, focused, determined and confident.

b. They are naturally inclined to be comfortable when in charge and naturally gravitate toward roles enabling them to lead.

c. They prefer to call the shots and tell others what to do, not because they love to be bossy, but because they love to get things done. The more people are working together on a project, the faster the task will be accomplished.

d. They have a high drive for achievement. They want to do something of significance that lasts well beyond their lifetime. They want to leave a mark on this world for others to see.

10. High I:

a. People that score high on the I scale are charismatic, outgoing, engaging, inspiring, enthusiastic.

b. They are built to shake paradigms; to sift people's thinking to a whole new perspective. They love to help people break free and step into a new area of freedom.

c. They are very comfortable with the microphone and the spotlight. They have plenty to share and look for opportunities to influence others toward a common goal.

d. Freedom is continuously urging them to step outside of restrictions and into great levels of freedom. They naturally avoid restraints, limitations and anything that would keep them from being able to fully "stretch their wings" and experience life in full.

11. High S:

a. People that score high on the S scale are stable, patient, loyal and service oriented.

b. They enjoy helping and supporting others. They derive a good deal of satisfaction in life knowing that they added value to another person's life.

c. On teams, these people are the glue that helps hold them all together. They are connected with the rest of the team and have a great sense as to how everyone is really doing.

d. They are easy to get along with and are natural peacemakers.

12. High C:

a. People that score high on the C scale are detailed, planners, deliberative, analytical and careful.

b. They love information. The more the better. They consume it in a never-ending quest to have the right answer and to create the right solution.

c. Arguing with a High C is typically futile, as they have researched everything about what you are arguing about and chances are that you are completely wrong. (Followed by laughter???)

d. They are comfortable handling very detailed tasks and carry them out time and time again with great results. They create systems for these detailed tasks to make sure everything is done correctly.

13. The next step is to have everyone identify their primary DISC style. There are several different ways to do this:

a. Have everyone in advance complete an online DISC Assessment (There are free and paid versions).

b. Pass out a paper version for everyone to complete.

c. Use the following descriptions to help them identify their own likely style: Ask everyone to think about the four types that you just described and think about the one style that best describes their set of behaviors. Many will be able to identify with two or more styles, but try to pick the one that best describes you then raise your hand when have selected one. We are now going to go through a series of steps to double check your choice before we move forward.

- ¤ Raise your left hand if you generally approach situations with a task and detail oriented approach or raise your right hand if you generally approach situations with a people and relationship focused approach.
- ¤ Now raise your left hand if you are generally more active, faced paced and bold in approaching new problems or raise your right hand if you are generally more thoughtful, moderate paced and careful in approaching new problems.

d. Now let's add up the hand signals and see how well they match up with your best guess after going through the list of the four DISC styles:

- ¤ If you raised your left hand twice, then you are likely a high D.
- ¤ If you first raised your left hand and then your right hand, you are likely a high C.
- ¤ If you raised your right hand twice, then you are likely a high S.
- ¤ If you first raised your right hand and then your left hand, you are likely a high I.

14. Now you have two quick ways to help you identify your primary DISC type. If your initial guess and the hand signaling match, you've got a great idea of your actual style.

15. If the two didn't match, one is likely your primary type and the other is your secondary type. For the rest of the workshop, you can choose which is your primary DISC type to participate in the following activities.

16. It is important to remember that no one is just a high I, high C, high S or high D. Everyone is a combination of all of the types and has the capability of behaving in whatever way they choose to, whenever they choose.

17. Conclude by discussing that none of the four types are inherently right or wrong. All are valuable and necessary for the world to function well.

18. A well-balanced organization needs to have powerful people that represent each of the four areas while having a voice that contributes to the team's future. When they add their own unique perspective, each adds additional strength to help ensure the continued success of the team.

19. Your primary DISC type does not define who you are or what you can do. It highlights your behavioral tendencies. You are responsible for your actions and behaviors — so choose them wisely!

20. Maturity in DISC doesn't look like someone that scores 100% in all four scales, nor do they have each scale even at the 50% midline. Maturity is to understand your style with its strengths and limitations and to intentionally work with others who have different strengths to build interdependent relationships that benefit everyone involved.

Alternate Options: This is a great place to start. As you feel more comfortable leading workshops, start adding in and making changes so it becomes your presentation. Characters from popular media can help the audience create a grid for each DISC type. Examples could include Maximus from the movie Gladiator for the High D. Jim Carey, the comedian, for the High I. Mother Theresa, the humanitarian, for the High S and Sherlock Holmes, the fictional detective, for the High C. When you are ready to add in projectors and slides, you can include pictures or short video clips to help characterize the figures. Be sure to follow all copyright regulations.

Tips: Participants can hold a lot of anxiety over their type. Depending upon their past experience with DISC, some may feel that some types are more valuable than others. In Western cultures, outgoing types can be seen as more advantageous or desirable because those types are highlighted in movies and tv shows.   How you present these four types can help everyone to accept and become excited about their type. My hope is that you present each type so compellingly that everyone would want to be the type you are currently presenting!

REINFORCING EXERCISES

Training with DISC

IDEAL VEHICLE

Purpose: To identify differences in thought processes and values.

Overview: Have the participants break up into their primary DISC type groups with 6-12 in each group depending upon the size of the audience. They will work together to answer the following questions about their primary DISC type:

- List 3 adjectives to describe your primary DISC type
- What kind of vehicle would that type buy if money were no object and why?

- What color vehicle would that type get and why?
- What qualities of the vehicle would they like most and why?
- What would their bumper sticker say?

Prerequisite: Each person should know their primary DISC type.

Materials: None. But you may consider projecting the questions on a screen, writing them on a whiteboard or printing them on a handout.

Preparation: Possibly. (See suggestions above.)

Time: 35 minutes.

Time Line: 5 minutes – Introduce exercise and break into groups.

10 minutes – Time to answer the questions.

10 minutes – Team presentations.

10 minutes – Wrap up.

Instructions:

1. Ask the participants to break up into their primary DISC type groups with 4-12 in each team.

2. Tell them that they will work together to respond on behalf of everyone that has their same type as to the ideal vehicle they would want.

3. As a team they will answer the questions and then select a representative to share the answers with everyone else.

4. After they meet as a group to answer the questions, bring the representatives from each group up to the front.

5. Have the High D team go first followed by the High S team. Then the High C team followed by the High I team.

6. Follow up by mentioning highlights from each of the teams, noting the differences and similarities.

Alternate Options: If the audience understands each type well enough, you can randomly assign groups together and then designate each group a different primary DISC type. Be sure to give ground rules to honor each type when presenting the answers so that the laughter does not turn into mocking. This can work for smaller groups that do not have several participants in each type group. You can also ask them to draw the vehicle on the back of the paper.

Tips: Focus on helping everyone to have a good time without poking fun at other types.

Training with DISC

D I S C
R E V I E W

Purpose: Engage participants in the learning process with a teach-to-learn approach.

Overview: Break the group up into evenly distributed mixed type teams of 4. The group assigns a DISC type to each person and then they have one minute to study before teaching the group about that type.

Prerequisite: Previous training of each DISC type.

Materials: None.

Preparation: None.

Time: 20 minutes.

Time Line: 5 minutes – Introduce exercise and break into groups of four.

3 minutes – Prepare for presentations.

10 minutes – Group presents to itself (2 minutes each).

7 minutes – Debrief.

Instructions:

1. Ask everyone to stand up and get into a group of four.

2. Have every group assign each person as either D, I, S or C. Ideally they should not be assigned as their primary style, but it is ok when that happens.

3. They will have three minutes to review their notes before teaching about that behavioral style for two minutes.

4. Allow them time to assign the roles before starting the three-minute timer to study their assigned type.

5. Give two minutes for them to share about each type before switching to the next presenter in the group.

6. After retuning to their seats, ask them what they got out of this exercise. What did they learn? How well do they know that type now?

Alternate Options: You can ask that each person teach on a type that is not their own unless the entire group has the same DISC type.

You could split the participants into four groups and have them build a presentation together and share with everyone from the front.

Tips: If some groups end up with five people, have two people team up to present together.

Training with DISC

DIFFICULT DEALINGS

Purpose: Create a direct application to what is being learned about the different types as well as increasing communication and team building.

Overview: Everyone identifies three people they would like to improve communication with. Answer four pre-defined questions for each one. Then discuss strategy to improve communication with another participant.

Prerequisite: Understanding of all four primary types. Understanding of each type's motivators and anxiety producers.

Materials: None. But you may consider projecting the questions, writing them on a whiteboard or printing them on a handout.

Preparation: Possibly. (See suggestions above.)

Time: 35 minutes

Time Line: 3 minutes – Introduce exercise.

12 minutes – Identify three people and answer the questions.

10 minutes – Share strategies with someone else.

10 minutes – Group interaction.

Instructions:

1. Discuss the value of communication in everyday life and how misunderstandings can cause large rifts in friendships and family relationships.

2. Improving communication starts with listening to the other person and trying to understand their point of view.

3. As individuals, have everyone identify three people in their personal lives they would like to improve communication with. Have them answer the following questions once for each of those people. Questions:

   a. What does an interaction with them typically look like?

   b. What is likely that person's DISC type?

   c. What are their motivators and anxiety producers?

    d. How can you approach them differently to try to create a different outcome?

4. Have the participants find someone they don't know well and share, not the names, but the strategies they wrote out. Encourage them to share feedback and suggestions as well as encouragement with each other.

5. Conclude by asking a few people to share their strategies and when they hope to first implement them.

Alternate Options: This exercise works well in a reconcilliation process between people that have problems with each other or with groups that aren't getting along well. Suggesting each person picks three people from the other team they least get along with can begin to create bridgeways to improved communication and connection.

Tips: Question three can be answered in advance either by a training session that you do, or by first using the exercise titled Motivators and Anxiety Producers. Some DISC Assessment results include the same information. I have also included that information in the DISC Workshop participant workbook titled The Essential DISC Training Workbook.

Training with DISC

BUILDERS
AND
FINISHERS

Purpose: To further everyone's understanding of different approaches to risk, patience and opportunities.

Overview: Assign teams as either 'Builders' or 'Finishers.' They work as a team to create a presentation as to why their type is best. Builders are the pioneers and Finishers are the refiners. Teams brainstorm together and then send representatives to share their presentation. Share ground rules and summarize the presentations, highlighting the value of each approach.

Prerequisite: None.

Materials: None.

Preparation: None.

Time: 45 minutes.

Time Line: 5 minutes – Introduce exercise and break into groups.

       15 minutes – Group discussion.

       10 minutes – Presentations.

       15 minutes – Group discussion.

Instructions:

1. Break the group up into evenly distributed mixed type groups of 4-12.

2. Assign teams as either Builders or Finishers.

3. Give analogy of building a house. A team comes out to prepare the ground, sets the foundation, lines out the rooms, sets in the electrical lines and plumbing and then frames the house. After the walls and roof are up, another team comes and makes the home livable with walls, carpet, cabinets and sinks.

4. Just like with a house, Builders are the ones that break ground first and strive to be at the cutting edge with new ideas, projects and accomplishments that others thought were impossible.

5. Finishers are the ones that see potential in other's work and build in features and options for driving up the value of the initial idea and bringing it to new levels of excellence.

6. Give them 15 minutes to prepare their presentation as to why their assigned type is best.

7. Set ground rules of honoring others, not using contrasts to compare as this is a preference, not a moral right our wrong.

8. Bring up presenters to share their team's arguments; follow each by applause.

9. Conclude by asking questions of each team about whether they agreed with their team's assigned type and why or why not. Was it easy or hard to create arguments for the assigned type?

10. Ask for examples of how some have been pioneers and others have been finishers.

11. Summarize the value of each type and how each one benefits from the breakthrough the other generates.

Alternate Options: You can break up the teams by primary DISC type, or by grouping Ds with Is and Ss with Cs or to make it a little more interesting you could group Ds with Ss and Is with Cs.

Tips: Setting the ground rules early in the process can help to ensure everyone enjoys this exercise and comes away with a greater appreciation for the value another style brings.

One might think that the Ds and Is are all Builders and the Ss and Cs are all Finishers, but I have not found that to be true. There may be a high percentage, but not as high as one might think.

Training with DISC

HOW WE
ARE
MISUNDERSTOOD

Purpose: To reveal the misperceptions of each type and create new paradigms for seeing the best in each type.

Overview: Have the participants break up into their primary DISC type groups with up to 12 in each group depending upon the size of the audience. Each group prepares a presentation of the ways in which their type is misunderstood. For each area where their type is commonly misunderstood, have the team include what their intentions really are and how they would prefer to be perceived. Each group presents. Finish with discussion and highlighting points from each type.

Prerequisite: None.

Materials: None.

Preparation: None.

Time: 45 minutes.

Time Line: 5 minutes – Introduce exercise and break into groups.

15 minutes – Group discussion.

10 minutes – Presentations.

15 minutes – Group discussion.

Instructions:

1. Ask the participants to break up into their primary DISC type groups with 6-12 in each team.

2. Share with them that the objective is to work as a group to identify how and when their type is commonly misunderstood and where others misinterpret actions. Not only will they share how they are misunderstood, but what their real intentions are and how they would prefer to be received.

3. After 15 minutes of preparation time, presenters will come up and share. Ds first followed by Ss, Cs and then Is. Encourage the audience to take down notes for future reference.

4. Conclude by highlighting the key areas of misunderstanding and the real intentions during those times. Ask for feedback on how they can use this information to improve connections with staff and family.

Alternate Options: Allow participants to ask questions of the presenters.

Tips: There are several "Aha" moments that can happen as the audience hears different groups present and they think about personal experiences with coworkers and family. When these moments are shared, learning and participation increase.

TRAINING WITH DISC 26

MARKETING TEAM

Purpose: Team participation, sales/marketing team development, or just to reinforce understanding of the other DISC types.

Overview: Have DISC type groups select an object in the room that they can carry. After selecting it, they will develop and present a marketing pitch aimed at their opposite DISC type.

Prerequisite: Previous training on the four DISC types including the drivers of each type. Communication Style training is helpful as well.

Materials: Objects in the room that can be easily held.

Preparation: Ensure the room has several moveable objects for the participants to use in the exercise.

Time: 45

Time Line: 5 minutes – Introduce exercise and break into groups.

        15 minutes – Group discussion.

        25 minutes - Presentations & group discussion.

Instructions:

1. Have the participants break up into their primary DISC type groups with 6-12 in each group depending upon the size of the audience.

2. Share with them that even if you never work for a marketing company, everyone is a sales person. They are always selling a project proposal, a suggestion, a resume or themselves to others.

3. Your group will have 15 minutes to find an object in the room that they can carry and will work as a team to create a presentation aimed at their target market.

4. Ds will sell to Ss and Ss to the Ds. Is will sell to Cs and the Cs will sell to the Is.

5. You will want to think about how your customer thinks, what drives them and their communication style.

6. After each presentation, you will highlight what they did well to present to the other type.

7. Conclude by asking for what the presenters did well and how participants can use this thought process to sell their next project or suggestion.

Alternate Options: You can carefully select one person as a representative from each DISC type to be the representative of the audience to ask how they felt about the presentation and how motivated they were to purchase the product. These representatives should be prepped to be positive and to focus most on what the team did well.

Tips: This is not a competition. This is a fun-filled and energizing exercise to help groups focus on how the other types communicate. Encourage teams to honor everyone in the room, especially their customers!

Training with DISC

BLIND
SPOTS

Purpose: To get types thinking about their style and when a strength ceases to benefit them and can slow them down. Also helps identify ways other groups can help them overcome those blind spots.

Overview: Allow them time to talk and discuss the shortcomings their type might encounter, or that have the possibility of disappointing others. Then they can share their results with the rest of the participants along with ideas of how others can help them overcome these blind spots.

Prerequisite: Understanding of their primary type.

Materials: None.

Preparation: None.

Time: 45 minutes.

Time Line: 5 minutes – Introduce exercise and break into groups.

      15 minutes – Group discussion.

      10 minutes – Presentations.

      15 minutes - Group discussion.

Instructions:

1. Have the participants break up into their primary DISC type groups with 6-12 in each group depending upon the size of the audience.

2. Share that leaders can sometimes have huge blind spots or faults that they aren't aware of. Some happen when our strengths are over used and others happen because of a weakness.

3. Have the team work together to identify areas where they, as leaders (at work, home, life), may have blind spots and weaknesses.

4. Present to the audience the team's findings along with suggestions on how other co-leaders can help them see their blind spots and begin to address them.

5. Conclude the session by summarizing the points and asking the audience questions about how they have felt or might feel trying to help a co-leader with an obvious blind spot.

Alternate Options: You can also assign each team a primary DISC type to think about, discuss and then present the shortcomings of serving under that type of leader.

Tips: If some in your group have difficulty thinking about themselves in a leadership role, ask them to think about how they would lead if today they were put in charge of a 10 person team. Apart from inexperience, how could their strengths be overused? Were would their weaknesses show up?

Training with DISC

ACCOUNTABILITY
PARTNERS

Purpose: Reveal the value of creating accountability partnerships.

Overview: Ask the audience to complete a set of questions before getting in groups of three to get to know each other and create an accountability plan to help pursue personal goals after the workshop ends.

Prerequisite: None.

Materials: None.

Preparation: None.

Time: 25 minutes.

Time Line: 5 minutes –Introduce exercise.

   5 minutes – Individuals answer questions.

   15 minutes – Group discussion.

Instructions:

1. Please write down your answers to the following questions:
   - 1.   What value can DISC bring to the team?
   - 2.   What is the biggest take-away that you've learned about so far?
   - 3.   How does understanding your own style help you connect with others?
   - 4.   Who needed this workshop more, you or the people sitting next to you?
   - 5.   What two things have you learned so far that could improve connections with others?
   - 6.   What do you need most to help implement what you are learning?

2. Break up into groups of three with individuals that you either don't know, or don't know well and review your responses.

3. Ask each other the following questions:

   a. If I were to partner with you to help implement what you are learning, how could I best encourage and support you?

   b. What would you like to have accomplished in two weeks that I can celebrate with you?

   c. If I called/emailed you in three weeks to hear about the progress you've made, what question(s) would you like me to ask you?

Alternate Options: You can allow the accountability groups to form on their own, or you can intentionally mix them up to ensure that there is a variety of DISC types in each group, or that they are from different departments or groups to encourage different connections.

Tips: Accountabilty groups work best in groups of three to five. Larger groups can have difficulties finding times to connect and smaller groups can easily disintegrate into nothingness.

VALUABLE

Purpose: Encourage everyone to value their style and what helps them to stand out and understand the contribution they bring to others.

Overview: Have DISC type groups create a list of 7-10 ways in which their type is amazing and where they bring value. Then have them repeat this process for the other three DISC types. Bring an entire DISC type group to the front and have the audience read off ten different ways that the other types see them as valuable.

Prerequisite: Previous training on the four DISC types.

Materials: None.

Preparation: None.

Time: 40 minutes.

Time Line: 5 minutes – Introduce exercise and break into groups.

15 minutes – Group discussion.

20 minutes – Presentations.

Instructions:

1. Have the participants break up into their primary DISC type groups with 6-12 in each group depending upon the size of the audience.

2. Work together as a team to create a list of seven to ten statements that represent what is amazing, significant and valuable about your type that everyone should know.

3. Then repeat that process for the other three DISC types.

4. Have all of the Ds come up to the front and then have the audience read nine of the statements that they created about how valuable they are.

5. Thank the Ds for being so valuable and have the audience applaud them before they sit down.

6. Repeat this process for the Ss, the Cs and finally the Is.

Alternate Options: You can pull the nine statements from the audience as a whole or you can ask that each DISC type group shares three statements each.

Tips: I prefer the presentation order to start with the Ds and end with the Is. When the Ds go first the Is, who love to be encouragers, remain in the audience. The Ss and Cs get a feel for the process and momentum builds to see everyone share how valuable the Is are.

C O A T
OF
A R M S

Purpose: To reinforce knowledge of participant's own style and help people work together.

Overview: DISC type groups create a coat of arms on a poster board to present to the audience sharing how the symbolism and colors represent some dynamic of their DISC type.

Prerequisite: Previous training on the four DISC types.

Materials: Large poster board and a colored marker set for each group of 6-12.

Preparation: Separate out poster boards and pen sets for each group.

Time: 45 Minutes

Time Line: 5 minutes – Introduce exercise and break into groups.

15 minutes – Groups plan and create their crest.

20 minutes – Each DISC type group to share the symbolism of their crest to the audience. (Add more time for larger groups).

5 minutes – Group discussion.

Instructions:

1. Have the participants break up into their primary DISC type groups with 6-12 in each group depending upon the size of the audience.

2. Share about how armies and knights were identified by a Coat of Arms. This would be displayed on tunics and shields. The symbols and colors each represented something about that group.

3. As a group you will create your own coat of arms to display to the audience and share what each part means as a way to demonstrate what your type does best.

4. Give them 15 minutes to discuss and draw out the coat of arms.

5. Invite representatives to the front to share the symbolism to everyone afterwards.

Alternate Options: You could purchase plain white XL t-shirts for the teams to decorate and then allow someone from the team to model the shirt while the spokesperson discusses the significance of the decorations.

Tips: Adding in a ground rule can help ensure that no one leaves the exercise feeling unhappy. Before the groups explain their crest, remind them that honor was an essential qualification for knights so when explaining each crest, be sure to not use language that puts down or casts a negative contrast toward another type.   Simply focus on the positives of your type.

Training with DISC

DREAM
JOB

Purpose: Identify the aspects of each type's dream job to identify what brings them happiness.

Overview: Have DISC type teams discuss aspects about their dream jobs

The focus is less on what they will actually do, and more on what aspects of that job appeal to them the most.

Prerequisite: None.

Materials: None.

Preparation: None. But you may consider projecting the questions, writing them on a whiteboard or printing them on a handout.

Time: 45 Minutes

Time Line: 5 minutes – Introduce exercise.

> 10 minutes – Individuals think about and write down the aspects of their dream job.

> 20 minutes – Split into DISC type groups and discuss their answers to find common points.

> 5 minutes – Group discussion.

Instructions:

1. Discuss that very few people are currently working in their dream jobs. Identifying what makes up a dream job is the best place to start. This process will help you to identify not what you will do, but what aspects of the job fit best for you and your DISC type.

2. Give participants ten minutes to respond to the questions below on their own.

    ▫ 1.   What motivates and demotivates?

    ▫ 2.   List five aspects of the ideal work environment and why they are important.

    ▫ 3.   Describe your ideal boss and the least desirable aspects of a boss.

    ▫ 4.   How can others provide encouragement in the middle of a frustrating problem.

    ▫ 5.   How much time is spent interacting with others versus getting work done?

    ▫ 6.   What type of pace would you prefer?

    ▫ 7.   How is conflict handled?

    □ 8.   Do you prefer things to change around frequently or not? Why?

3.   Have the participants break up into their primary DISC type groups with 6-12 in each group depending upon the size of the audience.

4.   Give them 20 minutes of group discussion to share what similarities and what differences they had in their responses.

5.   Allow for five minutes of group discussion for types to share a few of their key dream job aspects and highlight similarities and differences.

Alternate Options: You could also have groups present their findings. This would enhance the other group's understanding of how each type would like to be treated as an employee.

Tips: Before using this exercise in an organization, find out if the results will be used to create change. If that isn't an option, I would steer to another exercise.

Training with DISC

MOTIVATORS AND ANXIETY PRODUCERS

Purpose: Identify each type's motivating factors and anxiety producers.

Overview: DISC type groups discuss and create a list of three things that motivate them and three things that can increase the group's anxiety. Then these items are shared with the entire group.

Prerequisite: None.

Materials: None.

Preparation: None.

Time: 45 minutes.

Time Line: 5 minutes – Introduce exercise and break into groups.

> 15 minutes – Each group to discuss and list out motivators and anxiety producers.

> 20 minutes – Each DISC type groups share their list.

> 5 minutes – Group discussion.

Instructions:

1. Have the participants break up into their primary DISC type groups with 6-12 in each group depending upon the size of the audience.

2. Instruct them to work as a team to identify the underlying motivators that help drive their behaviors.

3. Have them also create a list of what things cause the most anxiety in their type and why.

4. They will then share with the rest of the group the top three motivators and the top three anxiety producers for their DISC type. Each item should include a brief explanation or example to help the audience understand.

Alternate Options: If your group really understands each of the four DISC types, you could assign each group to create a list of motivators and anxiety producers for a different DISC type.

Tips: Here are some of the commonly discussed motivators and anxiety producers for the DISC types:

- Motivators:
  - D = Significance, Importance
  - I = Embraced, Freedom

- □ S = Connection, Stability
- □ C = Excellence, Expertise.
- Anxiety Producers
  - □ D = Insignificance, Controlled
  - □ I = Rejection, Boxed In
  - □ S = Disconnection, Conflict
  - □ C = Failing, Being Wrong.

TRAINING
WITH
DISC
33

LEADERSHIP
SCENARIO

Purpose: To understand different leadership types between the four types including speed of decisions and levels of compassion.

Overview: Small type groups each work to find a solution to a difficult problem. The audience walks around listening to the process, takes notes and shares them after the teams deliver their answer.

Prerequisite: None.

Materials: Two printed pages for each team of the leadership scenario problem.

Preparation: Printing out copies of the leadership scenario problem.

Time: 45 minutes.

Time Line: 5 minutes – Introduce exercise and break into groups.

10 minutes - Each group to discuss and create a solution to the problem.

15 minutes – Each DISC type team to share their answer to the problem.

15 minutes – Group discussion.

Instructions:

1. Assign three to four participants from each primary DISC type collect into DISC type groups around separate tables. The rest of the audience is assigned as silent observers.

2. Share the Leadership Scenario problem with everyone.

3. Instruct the observers that they must refrain from talking during the team discussions. They are only to take notes and answer the questions listed below, which will be discussed at the end.

4. Instruct the four DISC teams that they will have 10 minutes to discuss in their own groups, the scenario, and create a solution that they will share with everyone afterwards.

5. Scenario:
   - You are the owner of a business that has been in your family for over 50 years. Growth has slowed in the last three years and now half of your long-standing customer contracts have not been

renewed this year. Your personal and business loans are coming due and you need to come up with $20,000 in the next three months or face bankruptcy, foreclosure on the facility's lease and termination of 65 staff.

▫ You've been reluctantly taking a $20,000 per quarter salary, but only because you've exhausted your personal savings and are caring for your aging parents. You are the face and personality of the company and the reason for its success in the past. If you didn't take your salary, you could pay off the business debts, but would loose your own house, which your family loves.

▫ Your General Manager earns $15,000 per quarter. She has been working with you for 10 years and is well liked by the staff. Unfortunately, she has been caring for a critically sick child and must leave work regularly for one to two hours at a time. This has brought stress upon the Assistant Manager who then needs to cover the General Manager's responsibilities as well as his own.

▫ The Assistant Manager earns $12,000 per quarter. He has been with you for three years. He has done his job well, and has covered for the General Manager with a good attitude, but you can tell he has several areas yet to grow in to really handle that role.

▫ Your top salesperson also earns $12,000/quarter. She consistently produces two to three times more sales than any other salesperson. She is also crass and rude to other staff. No one wants to work with her or hear her brag about being the best thing this company has going. She has been warned about her foul language, but you know it continues anyway. Everyone would love to see her go, but her sales have been keeping the company from loosing more money.

- In 30 days you are having your annual employee family dinner. Staff in your small town look forward to this all year long. It is the talk of the town, and staff and their entire family are proud to be part of it. You know that cancelling the event would save you $10,000, but would be a big blow to morale. On top of that, you could loose two contracts if you cancel this event with your two vendors that have contracts up for renewal.

6. Start the timer and have the four groups work on their own to come up with a solution. Allow the observers to silently walk around listening to each team and taking down notes to answer the following:

    - 1. What are some characteristics of the group process for each team?
    - 2. What aspects of the problem do they seem to focus more on? What do they miss?
    - 3. How well is the team communicating?
    - 4. What level of agreement did they achieve?

7. Bring up each group individually to present their solution.

8. Afterwards, ask the audience about their thoughts on the process and then go through the questions that you had them answer collecting information on all four of the groups.

9. Summarize the findings and highlight the different approaches of each team.

10. Focus on the benefit of a well rounded leadership team and the value each type brings to the table.

Alternate Options: Feel free to create your own scenario, or use one that correlates with something similar your audience has encountered or may encounter in their environment.

You can also switch things up halfway in the team decision process by having all but one person per team to go to different tables and designate the one person who stays as the team leader. Then ask the audience to re-answer all of their questions.

Tips: Encourage your observers to walk around the teams and listen in on each of them while taking notes. You may need to remind some of the observers that they are not to talk at all, even to each other. Some have a hard time not jumping in and running the show!

Training with DISC

PRIORITIES

Purpose: Highlight the different approaches of Ds and Cs versus Is and Ss.

Overview: Create groups made of a mix of Ds and Cs and other groups with a mix of Is and Ss. Have the Ds and Cs discuss the value of accomplishing tasks and the value to humanity it can bring. Have the Is and Ss discuss the value of building relationships and the value to humanity that can bring. Then bring up representatives from each group to share the findings.

Prerequisite: None.

Materials: None.

Preparation: None.

Time: 25 minutes.

Time Line: 5 minutes – Introduce exercise and break into groups.

10 minutes – Each group to discuss and prepare presentation on the value of accomplishing tasks or building relationships.

5 minutes – Both groups to share.

5 minutes – Group discussion.

Instructions:

1. Have the participants break up into two teams. One with just Ds and Cs and the other with just Is and Ss. If one team is really large, split it into smaller groups.

2. Instruct the group of Ds and Cs to discuss the value of accomplishing tasks and the value it brings to humanity. They will prepare a presentation to share with everyone.

3. Instruct the Is and Ss to discuss the value of building relationships and the value it brings to humanity.

4. Give them 10 minutes to discuss and prepare to present their case.

5. Set ground rules of honoring others, not using contrasts to compare as this is a preference, not a moral right or wrong.

Alternate Options: It may feel diabolical, but you could switch the instructions and have the Is and Ss discuss the value of accomplishing tasks and the value it brings to humanity and have the Ds and Cs discuss the value of building relationships and the value it brings to humanity.

Training with DISC

Tips: Setting the ground rules early in the process can help to ensure everyone enjoys this exercise and comes away with a greater appreciation for the value another style brings.

COMPLIMENT
FACE OFF

Purpose: Reinforce the value different types bring.

Overview: Have the participants break up into their primary DISC type groups with 6-12 in each group depending upon the size of the audience.

Each group is to create a list of the benefits the other type brings and is then to present those benefits to the other group (D-S or I-C) on stage facing each other. If groups are small, the entire team can come up. For large groups, each type group sends representatives.

Prerequisite: Previous training on the four DISC types.

Materials: None.

Preparation: None.

Time: 35 minutes.

Time Line: 5 minutes – Introduce exercise and break into groups.

10 minutes – Each group to discuss and prepare 10 compliments to share with the other team.

15 minutes – Group time to share.

5 minutes – Group discussion.

Instructions:

1. Have the participants break up into their primary DISC type groups with up to 12 in each group.

2. Instruct them to create a list of 10 benefits the other type brings. You can start their thinking process by sharing the following:

   a. Examples of ways that type has brought value to you or your team

   b. Value that type brings when difficult problems arise

   c. What would be missing if you did not have that type on the team

   d. Unique ways that type works and the value it brings

3. The Ds work on a list for the Ss and the Ss a list for the Ds. The Is work on a list for the Cs and the Cs for the Is.

4. Bring up the representatives from the Ds and ask the Ss to stand as the Ds deliver their list. Then have the Ss share while the Ds stand up. Follow with the Is

sharing while the Cs stand up and finally with the Cs presenting while the Is stand up.

5. Summarize the highlights and the value when different types work together with an expectation for different strengths to make things better.

Alternate Options: You can always mix up this exercise and randomly assign a different type to each group.

Tips: If a group gets stuck, have them think about personal experiences where the other type has added their strength to benefit them. You can also suggest they think about great people in the past that changed history.

CATCH UP TRAINING

Purpose: Reinforce what has been learned with a teach-to-learn style

Overview: Break up into pairs and summarize everything that the group has done and the key learnings as if the other person just arrived at the training.

Prerequisite: Previous training on DISC. The more previous training you've done the better this exercise works.

Materials: None.

Preparation: None.

Time: 20 minutes.

Time Line: 5 minutes – Introduce exercise.

5 minutes – Review notes and prepare teaching lesson.

5 minutes – Person one to teach person two.

5 minutes – Person two to teach person one.

Instructions:

1. Give everyone 10 minutes to look through their notes and prepare a five-minute teaching segment highlighting what was previously taught and summarize what the group learned through the exercises.

2. Provide five minutes for person one to teach person two.

3. Provide another five minutes for person two to teach person one.

Alternate Options: You can also ask someone to come to the front afterwards and share their review with the entire group. Alternately, you could assign person one to train on a particular subject and have person two teach on another one.

Tips: Briefly review the topics you have previously gone over. This exercise works great on follow up training since it allows them to think back to the original training and refresh each other's memory.

MANAGING TYPES

Purpose: To get a taste of the different approaches each style might make leading a team.

Overview: One leader from each DISC type will run through several exercises directing their team into various formations to win each contest and the title, Best Manager.

Prerequisite: None.

Materials: None.

Preparation: None.

Time: 20 minutes.

Time Line: 5 minutes – Introduce the exercise, select the leaders and organize the groups.

10 minutes – Run the events.

5 minutes – Celebrate the winner and have group discussion.

Instructions:

1. Select four leaders, one from each primary DISC type and have them come forward.

2. Randomly assign seven people to stand behind each leader. (4 for smaller groups)

3. Instruct them that the leaders can talk all of the time, but the rest of the team can only speak one at a time and only in response to a question from the leader.

4. The leaders are competing to find the best manager of the bunch by running through a few exercises. The leader with the most event wins will win the title of best manager.

5. Have the leaders organize their team in the following events:

    a. Line up in order of shortest to tallest.

    b. Line up in reverse alphabetical order by first name

    c. Group up by favorite color

    d. Set four people to make the letters Y, M, C and A and all others surround them with "jazz hands."

6. Keep track of the winners from each event and celebrate the winner with the title Best Manager. If there is a tie, run a standoff event where the team lines up by birth month.

7. Wrap up by asking for feedback from each of the leaders as to how they felt and what they did well and not so well.

8. Then ask the teams what they thought of the experience and what went well and what didn't.

9. Finish by asking the audience what they observed between the leaders.

Alternate Options: You can make the exercise a little more interesting by pulling the leaders out of the room when you give the instructions and do not allow them to share the objective of each race with the team.

You can also use a talking stick (pen) that allows each person to speak one-at-a-time. The leader must hold the stick first before it can be given to the next person.

Tips: This exercise can be used as an icebreaker, but I believe the group discussion Is more insightful when this exercise is done later in the training process.

Training with DISC

THE DISC CAR

Purpose: A fun way to highlight differences between the styles.

Overview: Break the group up into evenly distributed mixed type teams of 6-12. Break up into mixed type groups and create an analogy comparing the parts of a vehicle to DISC types. Present your results to the class sharing what DISC type is like what part and why.

Prerequisite: None.

Materials: None.

Preparation: None.

Time: 20 minutes.

Time Line: 5 minutes – Introduce exercise and break into groups.

10 minutes – Discussion and prepare the presentation.

10 minutes – Groups present.

5 minutes – Group discussion and vote on best analogy.

Instructions:

1. Break the group up into mixed type teams of 6-12.

2. Assign each group with the task of creating their own analogy to describe the four primary DISC types using the parts of a vehicle and how they work in harmony for the vehicle to work well.

3. Give the groups 10 minutes to create an analogy and prepare a presentation

4. Allow each team to present their analogy

5. Follow with group discussion and a show of hands to vote on the various analogies.

Alternate Options: You could supply pens and poster board and have the groups draw out their analogy highlighting the parts and notating the assigned DISC type.

Tips: Setting the ground rules early in the process can help to ensure everyone enjoys this exercise and comes away with a greater appreciation for the value another style brings. Also, the best analogy can become a tool you use in the future to teach about the DISC types.

PANEL
Q AND A

Purpose: To increase each type's knowledge about the other types.

Overview: Bring a group of the same type up to the front and allow the audience to ask questions about that type to better understand them.

Prerequisite: None.

Materials: None.

Preparation: None.

Time: 45 minutes.

Time Line: 5 minutes – Introduce exercise.

> 40 minutes – Each panel of Q&A (8 minutes of questions for each group, 2 minutes to thank the panel with applause and bring up a new panel.).

Instructions:

1. Inform everyone that you will be overseeing a Q&A panel and now is the time to find out everything you've ever wanted to know about each type and to find out what makes them tick.

2. Start by bringing up 4-8 high Ss to sit at the front of the room.

3. Invite the audience to raise their hand and as you select them, they ask a question.

4. After eight minutes, thank the Ss for coming up and then bring up 4-8 high Ds for another Q&A time. Repeat for the Cs and then the Is.

5.   You can start or add in any of the following questions to prime the process:

    a. How can other styles learn to better relate to you?

    b. How are you misunderstood?

    c. What are your fears?

    d. What is the value that you bring to a team?

    e. What does your leadership style look like?

    f. What do you have to be aware of with overusing your strengths?

    g. What drains you?

    h. What energizes you?

6. Conclude with an overview of the highlights from each group.

Alternate Options: You could pull one person from each DISC type up to the front and have each type answer each question that is asked. This method would give the audience a larger insight to the differences.

Tips: Establish ground rules that the question time should always be positive and encouraging and this is not the place to air frustrations about someone you know with that DISC type. Don't start questions with "Don't you..." or "You always..." or "You never...". Interrupt immediately if you feel tensions rise with a question or a response and rephrase the statement or ask a new question.

ANNOYING COMMUNICATION

Purpose: To highlight the different communication preferences.

Overview: Have the participants break up into their primary DISC type groups with 4-12 in each group depending upon the size of the audience. Ask each group to create a list of the top six communication errors others make in communicating with you. Then each group will present the list and include a specific example of poor communication and then a rephrased example in the group's preferred manner.

Prerequisite: None.

Materials: None.

Preparation: None.

Time: 45 minutes.

Time Line: 5 minutes – Introduce exercise and break into groups.

>15 minutes – Each group to discuss communication preferences and create list and examples.

>20 minutes – Each group to share for 4 minutes.

>5 minutes – Group discussion.

Instructions:

1.   Inform the group that they will be working on a communication exercise.

2.   Break the group up into mixed type teams of 6-12.

3.   Give them the instructions that each type has a different preferred method of communication. They are different because each way communicates in a way that meets a need.

4.   List out six of the top communication errors others make when communicating with you. These are the answers, questions and monologues that rub you the wrong way and can feel uncaring, ineffective, passive, drawn out and overly involved.

5.   Prepare to present this list to the rest of the group and include a brief specific example for each item on the list. Then include a second example that re-phrases the first to demonstrate your preferred method of communicating. Include the reasons why that way of communicating adds value to you.

6. You'll have fifteen minutes to discuss your type's communication preferences and create the list, the example, and the re-phrased example with reasons.

Alternate Options: You could gear this around a specific hot topic you know the group has, or a problematic area for them in the past.

Tips: Help everyone have fun without poking fun at other types.

Training with DISC

BONUS MATERIAL

Training with DISC

TRAINING WITH DISC 41

APPLICATION

Purpose: To establish a plan for how to implement what they learned and create lasting changes.

Overview: Have the participants think about all they have learned during the workshop and then create action steps to begin to walk them out. This helps to maximize the return on investment of their time and engergy spent in the workshop.

Prerequisite: None apart from a great workshop with tons of learning!

Materials: Blank note space. Slide or whiteboard listing the 5 questions listed in the instructions.

Preparation: Possibly with a whiteboard and pens or preparing a slide.

Time: 35 Minutes

Time Line: 5 minutes – Introduce exercise.

   5 minutes – Answer questions by themselves.

   20 minutes – Review answers in pairs.

   5 minutes – Group discussion.

Instructions:

1. Share that the vast majority of conference and workshop attendees never realize the fruit of their labor because they don't make a plan to implement those changes. All of their labor taking notes goes to waste as the binder collects dust, forgotten and abandoned. Those that see the most change and get the biggest return on their investment are the ones that create an action plan to use the information and keep it fresh in their minds.

2. Key questions to ask yourself include:
    - 1. What stands out the most from everything discussed in this workshop? Write out three or four items that stand out as areas where you feel an urgency to do something.
    - 2. Select two areas from the last question and think about what you would like to see happen in 60 to 90 days. Write out each goal as a sentence.
    - 3. Add to each goal a Time Line for accomplishing it and how you will know that you have accomplished each goal.
    - 4. Write down two action steps for each goal that will help you move forward to accomplish the goal.

Write them in response to the question, "What step will I take by when?"

- □ 5. What additional support, encouragement and accountability will help me reach my goals?

3. You will have 5 minutes to answer the questions on your own. You will then have 20 minutes to meet in a group of two or three to review answers to the questions and create a team or individual action plan. Afterwards I will ask for 3 or 4 people to share what about their goals and action plans with the class.

Alternate Options: During the group discussion time, you can also have them discuss at a table or group together into their departments or groups they came with. Add in additional time for larger group discussion time.

You can also withhold question five until they are meeting in their groups and then give them an additional five to ten minutes to help each other identify the support, encouragement and accountability needed to help each reach their goals. Additionally, you can suggest they share emails and calendar at a future time to connect and hold each other accountable for their action steps. Groups of three are ideal for this.

Tips: You can also integrate the Accountability Partners exercise with this one to create a poweful one-two punch!

Training with DISC

INTERRUPTING

Purpose: Breaking into a conversation is viewed in two very different ways by they different types. This exercise seeks to increase understanding around how to do this gracefully and with honor.

Overview: Break up into DISC Types with Ds and Is mixed together in groups of four to twelve and Ss and Cs mixed together in other groups of four to twelve. Have each team discuss what happens in a conversation when someone interrupts the other person and interjects their perspective on the topic.

- What does it do to the conversation?
- How do you, as the first speaker, feel when that happens?
- Why would someone interject when someone else is talking?

Prerequisite: None.

Materials: None.

Preparation: None.

Time: 15

Time Line: 5 minutes – Introduce exercise and break into groups.

5 minutes – Each group to discuss interrupting.

5 minutes – Presenters from the Ds and Is to share.

5 minutes – Presenters from the Ss and Cs to share.

10 minutes – Group discussion.

Instructions:

1. Inform the group that they will be working on a communication exercise.

2. Break the group up into teams of 6-12 with a mixture of Ds and Is in some groups and a mixture of Ss and Cs in other groups.

3. Share that different types view interruptions differently and an improperly done interruption can have a negative effect on the relationships, even when the interrupter had the best intentions.

4. Discuss in your groups how you feel when someone interrupts you when you are speaking and answer the following questions.

Training with DISC

    a. In general, how does it feel when someone interrupts me when I am speaking?

    b. When the interrupter cuts me off to discuss a different topic they would rather talk about, how do I feel?

    c. When the interrupter cuts me off to add value to the conversation how do I feel?

5. After the groups have had time to discuss the answers, ask the Ds and the Is each question and get one to two responses for each. Then ask the same questions to the Ss and Cs.

6. As the facilitator, summarize the answers from each of the two groups. Where Ss and Cs do not like to be interrupted and Ds and Is often enjoy it and the value it adds to make a great conversation.

7. Ask each of the types the following questions:

    a. How do you feel about interrupting someone who is speaking?

    b. If someone means well, and has something to add to the conversation, the best way to share it with the speaker is to do what?

    c. Have you ever been stuck in a conversation where they don't need anything from you except to hear their monologue that goes on and on and on? How long have you felt stuck? What did you do to break free? How did you feel afterwards?

8. As the facilitator, dialogue a bit about the how different groups feel about interruptions and the value honoring another's style can have. Ds and Is can wait a bit longer for an S or C to pause while Ss and Cs can confidently interject valuable information without feeling like they are being rude. When done with honor, communication is improved and relationships are grown.

Alternate Options: Even if you don't have time for this exercise, the lesson learned can be added into other interactive exercises to bring out the value of this powerful lesson. If you find yourself in an excited conversation where some participants are just jumping into the conversation on their own, it could be a great chance to highlight how Ds and Is are energized with helpful interruptions but Ss and Cs can view them as interruptive, distracting and dishonoring.

Tips: Try to find examples interruptions (or lack of interruptions) happening later in the workshop to point out and highlight to the group.

TRAINING WITH DISC **43**

QUICK REFERENCE

Purpose: To provide a reference point for the participant and those they work with and with family at home.

Overview: Complete the Quick Reference Guide downloaded from www.DISC-U.org/TrainingWithDISC and recommend that it be posted either at work or at home as a reminder to keep the information fresh in their mind and to help others be reminded of the best way to communicate and connect with the participant.

Prerequisite: Understanding of their DISC results to chart their graph and complete the sections

Materials: Printed Quick Reference Guides from DISC-U.org or make up your own.

Preparation: Print out or create your own Quick Reference Guide.

Time: 15 minutes.

Time Line: 5 minutes – Introduce exercise.

5 minutes – Complete Quick Reference Guide.

5 minutes – Discuss results with someone.

Instructions:

1. Pass out the printed Quick Reference Guide

2. Share that one of the ways to maximize what you've learned and help you improve connections and communication is to keep what you've learned at the front of your mind.

    a. This Quick Reference Guide is a great way to be reminded of your own style and that others have different ways to connect and communicate.

    b. When posted on a door at work or at home, it can let others know about you and remind them about your communication preferences.

    c. Spend a few minutes completing the different sections. Then you will find someone you don't know well and will share and discuss what you wrote down. Pretend the listener has never heard about DISC and share a few basics about what DISC is before you walk them through what each area of your Quick Reference Guide means.

LINKS AND RESOURCES

All of the resources mentioned in this book can be found at www.DISC-U.org/TrainingWithDISC.

I've included a list of any supplies that are discussed in the previous sections that mention or require materials.

Tips to Leading Great DISC Workshops

- DISC Assessment Options
- Pens
- Notebooks

- Training with DISC Handouts
- Particpant Workbook
- Projector
- Keynote / PowerPoint
- Screen
- Power Cords
- Audio/Video Cords
- Wireless Presenter
- Marketing Talent

General Workshop Items

- Timer
- Whiteboard Makers

Ice Breakers

- Tallest Tower Materials
  - Large Marshmallows
  - Coffee Stir Sticks
  - Plastic Table Cloth
  - Peppermint Starlights
- Blind Communication Materials
  - Colored Foam
  - Envelopes
  - Blindfold
- Lifeline
  - PVC Pipe Sections
  - Marble
  - Bucket

Reinforcing Exercises

- Coat of Arms
  - Large Poster Board
  - Colored Marker Set

DISC-U.org Resources

- The Essential DISC Training Workbook
- DISC Facilitator Training Kit
- Online Training

Additional DISC Resources

- Understanding You, Understanding Me, Wendy Crawford
- Taking Flight, Rosenburg & Silvert
- 8 Dimensions of Leadership, Sugerman, Scullard & Wilhelm
- The 4 Dimensional Manager, Straw

I'm excited to hear from you about your next workshop. Please feel free to email me with any questions as you are preparing for your workshop. I would also love to hear how well your workshop goes when implementing these exercises.

I can be reached at www.DISC-U.org or jasonh@DISC-U.org.

If you have other exercises or create variations of these and would like to share them with other DISC Facilitators for possible inclusion in another book like this one, send me a line. As our workshops improve so does the experience for all of our participants!

Made in the USA
Middletown, DE
09 November 2023

42285895R00110